A DAY IN THE LIFE WITH

HENLEY
AND HER PETS

A DAY IN THE LIFE WITH

HENLEY
and Her PETS

BY

Hollie Lynn

Xulon Press
555 Winderley Pl, Suite 225
Maitland, FL 32751
407.339.4217
www.xulonpress.com

Paperback ISBN-13: 978-1-66286-674-6
Hard Cover ISBN-13: 978-1-66289-417-6
eBook ISBN-13: 978-1-66286-675-3

First and foremost, I dedicate this book to God, my Heavenly Father, and to the Lord, Jesus Christ, my Savior. God is the Creator of Heaven and Earth and all who dwell therein and everything in it.

The Earth is the Lord's, and all it contains, the world, and those who live in it.
Psalm 24:1 (NASB)

I also dedicate this book to Henley, my precious granddaughter. Henley, I love you so much! You are a true gift from God! Thank you for all the ways you make me laugh and for the inspiration for this book. One day, you will grow up to be an amazing, woman of God! For now, you are an amazing, little girl . . . God's little princess! I sometimes miss the previous days when you said cute, made-up words and so much more. You are such a joy! You are the apple of God's eye. I look forward to watching you grow into the beautiful woman God has destined you to be.

Keep me as the apple of the eye; hide me in the shadow of Your wings.
Psalm 17:8 (NASB)

Hollie Lynn enjoys teaching God's Word to children. She has authored writings to include assisted a new author with her book. Most recently, Hollie authored, "A DAY IN THE LIFE WITH HENLEY and Her PETS." This book is mostly a real-life, story portraying what happens even in scary situations when we trust and believe God, and it shows how God demonstrates His love for us.

Visit us at: www.TrueHopeToday.com
Email Hollie at: hollie@truehopetoday.com

Hi everyone, my name is Henley. Today I am visiting my
Momma. She is my grandmother. I like to visit Momma.
We have so much fun together! Let me tell you about
some of the great fun at Momma's house.

Momma reads me the Bible and storybooks. Do you know, the Bible is the 'Word of God'? I like when Momma reads to me.

Momma and I also play together. A super, fun thing I like to do at Momma's is play with my puppy doggy, Keleigh, and kitty cat, Buddy. Keleigh and Buddy are so cute!

Keleigh likes to go outside and play with the squirrels and birds. Mostly, she likes to run and jump, and catch a frisbee.

Momma and I enjoy going outside and playing frisbee with Keleigh and watching her play with her little outside friends, the squirrels and birds. Keleigh also really likes to run past us, super-fast!

"Oh, look Momma, it looks like Keleigh is having so much fun talking to the squirrels. I think she said, 'Hello, Mr. and Mrs. Squirrel, it is a beautiful, bright sunny day. A good day to be outside and play. Will you play with me? We can have a race called Chase,'" Henley said with excitement.

"Henley, do you know that God created everything? He created you and I, and all the people. He created the animals and so much more," Momma shared. "Momma, I am so glad God made us and all the people! I am happy He made Keleigh and Buddy. Please tell me more about God," Henley said enthusiastically.

Everyone, I love God very much! I hope you do too.

Genesis 1:1 – 2:4 (NKJV) explains God's Creation in six days and on the seventh day, He rested.

So, God created man in His own image; in the image of God, He created him; male and female He created them. Genesis 1:27 (NKJV)

"Henley, we have been having so much fun talking about God and reading the Bible, we did not bring Keleigh in from outside. Please go to the door and call her to come in. It is time for Keleigh and Buddy to eat their supper. We also need to eat soon and get ready for bed," Momma explained.

"Yes, Momma. Keleigh might be very hungry from playing and running so much outside. Oh, no Momma, where is Keleigh? I do not see her in the yard," Henley screamed.

Momma said calmly, "We will go outside to see where she is. Look, Henley, somehow the gate became opened. I wonder if Keleigh was able to push it open. I do not see her anywhere."

Henley cried and stated, "Momma, I am so sad and afraid. I love Keleigh so much and I miss her. I want to find her now, but how?"

"Henley, just like when we pray and thank God for our food, and pray other times throughout the day, you can pray and ask God to protect Keleigh and help us find her," Momma replied.

"Okay, Momma, I will pray," said Henley.

Dear God, in Jesus' Name, Keleigh is missing. She was outside playing. We cannot find her. I am so sad and afraid. Please protect Keleigh and help us find her quickly. Amen!

"Alright, Henley, let's go look for Keleigh," Momma said.

Trust in the LORD with all your heart and lean not on your own understanding. In all your ways acknowledge Him, and He shall direct your paths. Proverbs 3:5-6 (NKJV)

Pray without ceasing. 1 Thessalonians 5:17 (KJV)

"Oh, Momma where is Keleigh? It is getting dark. I wish she would just bark and then we could hear her and find her," Henley said.

"Henley, I agree. We will continue to pray for Keleigh and trust God to protect her and return her to us quickly. It is getting late. We need to go home. Soon, it will be bedtime," Momma explained.

"I do not want to go home. Can we keep looking for Keleigh? Please, Momma, please!" Henley pleaded.

"Okay, we'll look a little longer," Momma replied.

"Henley, I hear barking. Look! There is Keleigh with that family. Oh, Keleigh, we found you! We missed you so much. You are jumping with much excitement to see us. We are so glad you are safe," Momma stated.

"Hello family! You found our dog, Keleigh. Thank you for taking care of her and keeping her safe! She got out of the yard. I do not have her collar and identification tag on her. That is wrong and I need to make sure she wears her collar. Again, thank you! Henley and Keleigh, we are going home now," Momma explained.

"Keleigh, I missed you so much! I was scared.
I am happy you are home. Please, do not leave again by
yourself. Momma said God created me and Momma and
everyone, and He created you and Buddy and all the
animals. I am so glad God created you and Buddy!
Oh, Keleigh and Buddy, you need to eat supper.
Please, go eat. Keleigh, you are such a nice puppy doggy!
Look, it is raining now. No more going outside tonight.
Not in the rain. You might get all soggy. I love you, Keleigh
and Buddy! Tomorrow, we will play and have fun,"
Henley said with great enthusiasm!

"Henley it is getting late. We had a long day.
It is time to read the Bible and pray. We need
to tell God, 'Thank you' for answering our prayers
about Keleigh," Momma said.

Henley replied, "Okay, Momma, I will pray."

Dear God, in the Name of Jesus, Thank-you for
protecting Keleigh and helping us find her and now
we are home safe. Please bless and protect me and
Momma, our family and friends, and Keleigh and Buddy.
Please give us good sleep tonight and help us to
have fun tomorrow with Keleigh and Buddy.
I love you, Jesus! You are Lord of all. Amen!

. . . Jesus Christ-He is Lord of all. Acts 10:36b (NKJV)

Everyone, do you know ... we need a Savior?

Because of Adam and Eve's sin in the Garden, we need a way back to God . . . a way to Heaven someday. Jesus is our, One and only Savior. He is the only way to God. The Bible says, "And there is salvation in no one else; for there is no other name under Heaven that has been given among mankind by which we must be saved." Acts 4:12 (NASB)

Genesis 3:1-24 (NKJV) explains why we need a Savior.

I, even I, am the LORD, and besides Me there is no Savior. Isaiah 43:11 (NKJV)

But God demonstrates His own love toward us, in that while we were still sinners, Christ died for us. Romans 5:8 (NKJV)

For God so loved the world that He gave His only begotten Son, that whoever believes in Him should not perish but have everlasting life. John 3:16 (NKJV)

Jesus is the only way to Heaven!

Then Jesus called a little child to Him, set him in the midst of them, and said, "Assuredly, I say to you, unless you are converted and become as little children, you will by no means enter the kingdom of heaven. Therefore, whoever humbles himself as this little child is the greatest in the kingdom of heaven." Matthew 18:2-4 (NKJV)

"Let not your heart be troubled; you believe in God, believe also in Me. In My Father's house are many mansions; if it were not so, I would have told you. I go to prepare a place for you. And if I go and prepare a place for you, I will come again and receive you to Myself; that where I am, there you may be also. And where I go you know, and the way you know." Thomas said to Him, "Lord, we do not know where You are going, and how can we know the way?" Jesus said to him, "I am the way, the truth, and the life. No one comes to the Father except through Me.'" John 14:1-6 (NKJV)

For I delivered to you first of all that which I also received: that Christ died for our sins according to the Scriptures, and that He was buried, and that He rose again the third day according to the Scriptures.
1 Corinthians 15:3-4 (NKJV)

That if you confess with your mouth the Lord Jesus and believe in your heart that God has raised Him from the dead, you will be saved. For with the heart one believes unto righteousness, and with the mouth confession is made unto salvation. Romans 10:9-10 (NKJV)

. . . Behold, now is the accepted time; behold, now is the day of salvation.
2 Corinthians 6:2b (KJV)

Everyone, have you asked Jesus to come live in your heart? If you have not, now is the time to. Believe in your heart and pray. You can pray like this. . . Dear Jesus, I know and believe God sent You to the earth. You suffered and died on the cross for my sins, and You rose again from the dead on the third day. I am sorry for my sins. I ask You to forgive all my sins. Please come and live in my heart. I want you to be my Lord and Savior. Jesus, I love You and I want to follow You all the days of my life. Please, God fill me with Your Holy Spirit. I ask You to help me to live for You and do good works for You always.
In Jesus' Name, Amen!

For we are His workmanship, created in Christ Jesus for good works, which God prepared beforehand that we should walk in them. Ephesians 2:10 (NKJV)

. . . And in Your book were written all the days that were ordained for me, when as yet there was not one of them. Psalm 139:16b (NASB)

Now that you've prayed and invited Jesus to live in your heart and to be Lord of your life, you are a new creation in Christ. The old has passed away and the new has come. If you and your family are not attending a church, you can all pray and ask God, in Jesus' Name, to lead you to the church He wants you to attend so you can grow strong in the Lord and learn more about God and His Holy Word. Remember, we told you the Bible is the Word of God. You are His and He is yours!

Therefore, if anyone is in Christ, this person is a new creation; the old things passed away; behold, new things have come.
2 Corinthians 5:17 (NASB)

My Beloved is mine, and I am His . . . Song of Songs 2:16a (NJKV)

I am my Beloved's, and my Beloved is mine . . .
Song of Songs 6:3a (NKJV)

Author's Note

It is always best for pets to wear a collar with an identification tag. Dogs and cats can also be microchipped, which can be helpful if they become missing. If a pet is missing, the pet can be located through an identification tag and/or a microchip. You can check with a veterinarian about a microchip. If you adopted your pet from an animal rescue or an animal shelter, they may be able to provide information about a microchip. Our dog, Keleigh, was safe and found. Please make sure your pets are always safe and wear proper identification.

Visit us at: www.TrueHopeToday.com

9 781662 894176